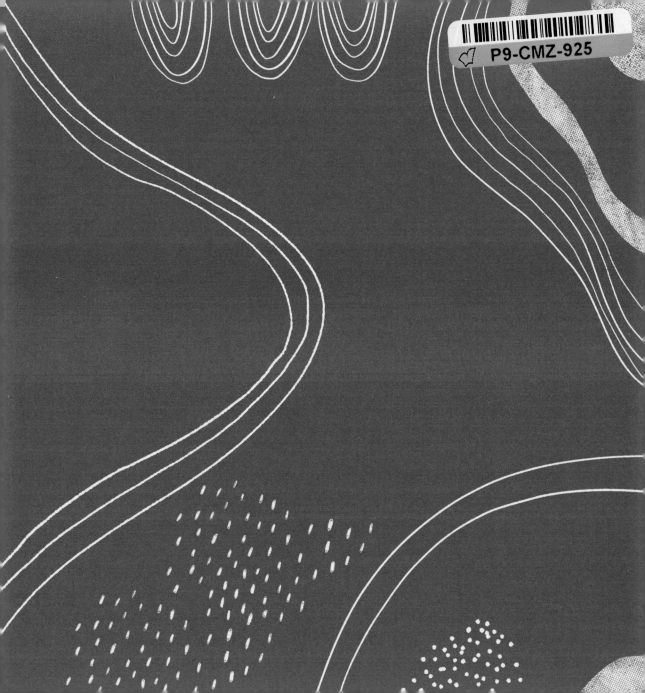

HERE'S TO YOUR RIDICULOUS LIFE

ADULTHOOD

IS LIKE LOOKING BOTH WAYS AND THEN GETTING HIT BY AN AIRPLANE. SO COME IN THROUGH THE BACK AND CLOSE THE FRONT DOOR THEN PULL UP A CHAIR AND SIT ON THE FLOOR. THIS IS COMPLETELY NONSENICAL, I'LL TELL YOU RIGHT NOW, KALAMZOO, REMARKABLE, AMUCK, AND BROWN COW.

READ TILL YOU LAUGH
OR READ TILL YOU CRY
HAVE FUN WITH THIS
BOOK, I BID YOU

BANZAI!

LIFE IS JUST TOO
DANG SHORT!
SO ALWAYS
.... THE
.... !

AND WHEN LIFE GIVES YOU .... MAKE ...., THROW IT AT ...., THEN RUN LIKE ....!

THE HARDER YOU

. . . .

THE LUCKIER YOU

. . . .

ME & YOU

AND A DOG NAMED

....

IF YOU WERE A ....,
YOU'D BE A

MONKEY'S

....

WHEN THINGS GET
ROUGH AND YOU
FALL ON YOUR

....,

RUB SOME.......................
ON IT AND KEEP
                        !
....

EVERY TIME

I

....,

I THINK OF

....

IF YOU

....

SO!

IF I COULD GIVE YOU THE **BIGGEST** TROPHY IN THE WORLD I WOULD!

IT WOULD BE .... FEET TALL

AND .... FEET WIDE!

IT WOULD HAVE

" .... "

ETCHED ACROSS THE BOTTOM,

AND THE TROPHY CUP

WOULD BE FULL OF

....

YOU PUT THE

....

IN MY

....

BUT SOMETIMES,
YOU ARE A

....

ON THE

OF

....

HUMANITY!!

IT'S SUPER

FUN

TO

....................——————....................

TILL YOU

....................————————....................!

AND IT'S SUPER

AWKWARD

TO ....

TILL YOU

....!

TWO'S A COMPANY;
A CROWD

NEVER LEAVE

....

WITHOUT

!
....

EAT, DRINK, AND BE

.... ,

FOR

TOMORROW

YOU MAY

....

SMILE LIKE YOU

....

CHEER LIKE YOU WON

....

BLUSH LIKE YOU

....

AND LAUGH

LIKE ....

IF A ....

WERE TO HIT

YOU IN THE FACE!

SOMETIMES,

YOU'RE AS CONFUSED

AS ....

IN A BAG FULL

OF ....

BUT SOMETIMES
ME TOO.
I GET COMPLETELY
TURNED AROUND
WHEN I _____!
AND ESPECIALLY
WHEN I _____.

LIFE IS

....

SO SMILE

WHILE YOU

STILL HAVE

....

LiFE iS ALSO

_____ !

AND iT'S _____

iF YOU'RE STUPiD.

WHEN THE GOING
GETS ....,
STOP
AND ....
THE ....!

A ....

A DAY

KEEPS THE

AWAY

ONE OF MY PREDICTIONS FOR YOUR FUTURE

IS THAT YOU'll OWN AT LEAST 10 ....,
15 CRAZY ....

A CLOSET FULL OF

....

AND MAYBE JUST 1

....

OR 2.

YOU CAN'T BUY

BUY

BUT YOU CAN
DEFINITELY BUY

EVEN THOUGH YOU'RE

iN ....,

YOU'RE ONLY ONE

.... AWAY

FROM KALAMAZOO.

PEOPLE SAY

IS

IMPOSSIBLE.

BUT I DO

EVERY DAY!

THAT AWKWARD MOMENT WHEN YOU'RE WEARING

AT ....

WHEN ALL ELSE FAILS, ADD A

IF YOU PUT _____ IN A BLENDER AND CRUSH IT UNTIL IT

_____ ,

IT MAKES FOR A

PERFECT

_____ -FILLED

WATER BALLOON.

YOU'RE A

....

IN MY

...........................!

YOUR ALWAYS KNOWS

WHAT'S UP!

SO TRUST THAT

WHEN LIFE TURNS ALL CATAWAMPUS

AND THE STARS ARE AT YOUR FEET AND THE SIDEWALK IS IN THE SKY ...

YOU JUST GOTTA

....

WITH THE

....,

ROLL WITH THE PUNCHES,
SING WITH THE ROOSTERS,
AND LAUGH WITH
THE CRAZIES!

THE GRASS IS ALWAYS

....

ON THE OTHER

....

& THE SNOW

IS ALWAYS ....

WHEN THERE'S A

.... AROUND.

IF YOU .... IT,

IT WILL ....

SOMETIMES YOU MAKE
ME FEEL SO

....

I COULD

....!

LIFE'S A

.... •

I MEAN, IT'S

A COMPLETE

.... •

is

BETTER

WHEN YOU'RE

.... iS GOOD

.... iS BETTER

.... iS BEST.

LiFE iS LiKE A BOX
OF ·····························.

OR A JAR OF

·····························.

AVOID _____

TO STAY ON THE

_____

OR JUST THROW
ALL CAUTION
TO THE
WIND
AND ....
IT ANYWAY.

NOBODY'S

....

ALL THE TIME.
LIKE SERIOUSLY
THAT WOULD BE
CRAZY OR ....

HAPPINESS
iS A WARM

AVOID THE

....

THAT KILLS

THE _____!

NEVER BE SO

....

THAT YOU DON'T

....•

WHEN AT FIRST

YOU DON'T

SUCCEED,

SIT DOWN AND EAT

A BIG PLATE OF

....

WITH A TALL GLASS OF

....

THEN TRY AGAIN!

KEEP ....

AND CARRY

A ....

BUT ALSO,
ALWAYS KEEP

....

AND CARRY
A WATER GUN!

_____ iT

UNTiL YOU

_____,

AND _____ iT

UNTiL YOU LAUGH!

IF YOU CAN'T
.................THEM,
THEM.
....

THEM THEN
DRIVE AWAY
FAST!

NEVER MISS A
GOOD CHANCE TO

....

iN THE

....

COOKIEJUICE

IS A COMBINATION OF CHOCOLATE CHIP COOKIES DIPPED IN ORANGE JUICE..

JUST AS WEIRD,
YOU & I
ARE A
COMBINATION
OF ....
AND ....

BEHIND EVERY GREAT

....

iS A ....

ROLLING THEIR EYES.

NEVER TRUST PEOPLE
WHO _____ I

IF YOU FIND
NOTHING IS
GOING RIGHT...

GO LEFT.

THEN MAYBE TURN ....

& DRIVE TO

....●

NEVER, EVER

GET STUCK iN FULL

.... MODE!

LiFE iS

_____

AND THEN

_____

NEVER PUT OFF _____ WHEN YOU CAN _____.

BUT ALWAYS PUT OFF

....

BECAUSE WHO'D
WANT TO DO THAT?

_____ iS THE SPiCE OF _____. JUST LiKE CiNNAMON iS THE SPiCE OF GREAT WAFFLES!

EVERY .... HAS A

SILVER LINING.

UNLESS iT'S A BATHTUB.
CAUSE THAT HAS A
.... LINING

YOU'RE AS COOL AS A

....

AND AS CALM AS A

....

YOU MOST CERTAINLY

CAN HAVE YOUR

....

AND......................iT TOO!

BASICALLY, YOU'RE

...................................•

AND I'M

...................................•

WHICH MEANS WE'RE BOTH PRETTY DANG

!

GIBBS SMITH
TO ENRICH AND INSPIRE HUMANKIND

24 23 22 21 20   5 4 3 2 1

Written by Kenzie Lynne, © 2020 Gibbs Smith

Illustrated by Erin MacEachern, © 2020 Erin MacEachern

Published by
Gibbs Smith
P.O. Box 667
Layton, Utah 84041

1.800.835.4993 orders
www.gibbs-smith.com

Designed by Erin MachEachern

Printed and bound in China
Gibbs Smith books are printed on either recycled, 100% post-consumer waste, FSC-certified papers or on paper produced from sustainable PEFC-certified forest/controlled wood source. Learn more at www.pefc.org.

ISBN: 978-1-4236-5452-0

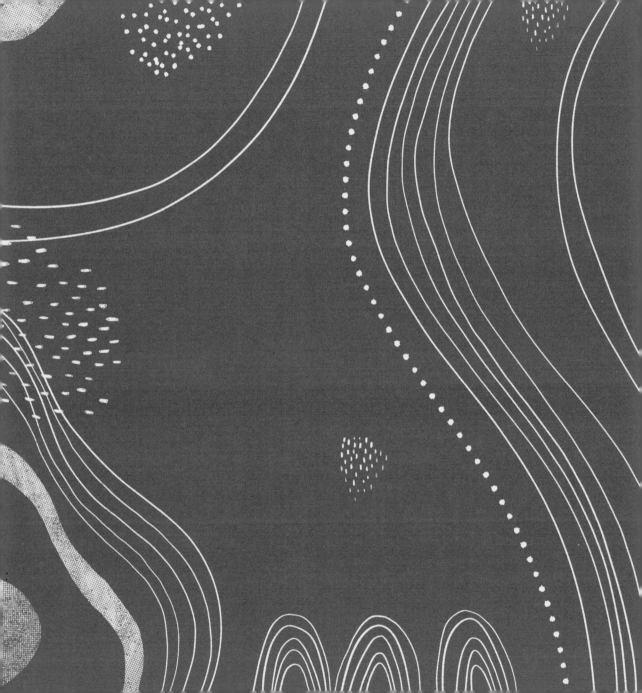